T0327883

New
Italian
Creative
Generation

NICG the series

NEW ITALIAN CREATIVE GENERATION

DAMIANI

I began writing about design in the magazines, *Modo* and *Domus* and talking about it using the medium of television with *Lezione di Design* (Rai Educational) and programs for Sky TV (*Case & Stili, design.book, A2*) along with producing work for the web and social networks.

In a process of personal transformation from critic to publisher (which does not necessarily rule out the critical aspect but implements it more loosely), I have discovered that there is no such thing as the perfect medium and that, paraphrasing the well-known adage, the medium does not always succeed in being a vehicle for the message.

Today, the internet is perhaps the word's medium of choice and yet the medium is necessarily so vast that the word can be difficult to find and to access.

The book endures as a validating and capable testimony. It is an artefact which can be interactive and dynamic, above all if it borrows methodology from other mediums and forms of expression. It is the case of this series, *New Italian Creative Generation*, which works on a renewed format that is similar to television or in any case, indebted to video which transforms the interview into a conversation with the corpus of the work of the protagonist subsequently illustrated in tables. A conversation, unlike an interview, leads the interlocutor to reveal himself as a person, as an individual (profile). At the same time, the author's questions act as a back-up, a speech-confession, able to avert a priori and ready-made answers implicit in standard questions which are often pre-packaged. The conversation is free but inflexible in terms of its space and time limits, and it is the author's ultimate testimony.

The message becomes unique, a tale, a narration, offering the reader a new, unexpected profile which is illustrative of the protagonist's work, precisely because it describes the person.

Giorgio Tartaro

NEW ITALIAN CREATIVE GENERATION | 01

Walter Vallini Architect
works 2000 | 2012

Curated by Giorgio Tartaro

Art direction Adriana Toti

All photographs used by permission:
Francesco Arese Visconti
Margherita Bignamini
Borchi & Cozzi
Johnny Dell'Orto
Tea Giobbio
Fernando e Sergio Guerra
Davide Lovatti
Mads Mogensen
Adriano Pecchio

DAMIANI © 2013

[DAMIANI]

DAMIANI
Via Zanardi, 376
Tel +39 051 63 56 811
40131 Bologna - Italy
www.damianieditore.com
info@damianieditore.com

Printed in February 2013 by Grafiche Damiani, Italy

ISBN 978-88-6208-279-2

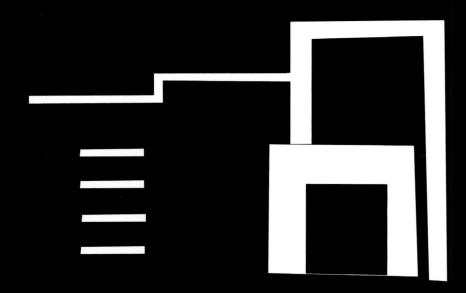

WALTER VALLINI ARCHITECT

Architect and artist/designer, Walter Vallini was born in Rome and studied in Florence. He now divides his time between Rome and Berlin.

Winner of the IDIA AWARDS in 1989, Vallini's work has been presented in numerous exhibitions and published by major magazines and publishing houses.

"Walter Vallini is an architect who practices design and art not as two separate practices, but as a single, self-sustaining activity. You could say that his works – tables, lamps, etc. – are items of furniture of great quality that could be called *Sculptures*, one of a kind pieces that are being made in serial production.

We prefer to reverse this train of thought: Vallini's sculptures are "functional" or "function-able", meaning sculptures that can also act as a lamp or table, but their essence consists in spatial constructions within a space, meaning sculptures."

Giorgio Bonomi

This book is the first in a series entitled "New Italian Creative Generation", directed by journalist and critic, Giorgio Tartaro, and dedicated to the most interesting Italian architects and designers of the last generation.

GIORGIO TARTARO
Walter Vattini

Walter, I would like to begin this conversation with you by asking about your formation, your university studies and your professional debut.

I studied in Florence, which I have always stressed as playing a very important part in my formation. Indeed, in Florence, while still a student, I had the opportunity to work in a bottega or workshop. It was the 'teaching workshop' of a professor who I believe to be a great architect, especially from the didactic point of view, even though he is not very well known by the general public. I am talking about Alessandro Gioli, one of the Florentine architects who, in the sixties, established the Ufo group, a group linked to the avant-garde movements of that period and especially to Radical Architecture.

This explains, in some sense, where your passion for art stems from.

As well as Gioli the Ufo group was made up of figures like Lapo Binazzi [...] This context generated a product design which had little to do with mass production, characterised by an approach aimed much more at producing a one-off: something closely resembling what I call "art design". Therefore, let's say that my foundations, my points of reference, were mapped during those years I spent studying at university in Florence under the person I consider to be my mentor. I believe studying architecture in Florence left me with a sort of imprinting, a particularly important mark that began to appear in my earliest works.

So you studied and graduated in Florence… and your professional debut?

After graduation I worked a great deal, mostly in interior design. As you well know I still haven't produced much architecture partly because in Italy it is one of the most complicated things in the world. Working on public projects is too complex. There is no problem getting into property speculation if you want but succeeding in producing works of architecture is a very difficult thing.

When you say you haven't produced much architecture what are you referring to? I seem to recall there was a winery.

I worked on the extension of a villa in the hills of Alba and then, yes, a winery with a barrique cellar and restaurant, which is, above all, a project involving the territory. The Langhe, extremely important in Italian tradition, is a territory that has been scarred by the speculation and shoddy building practices of the last forty years. Working in this context means shouldering an enormous sense of responsibility. There, this is what architecture is to me: an enormous sense of responsibility. An interior is an interlude, you can even afford to get it wrong, but for me architecture has an impact on a territory or on an urban context of structurally decisive importance.

a CONVERSATION

However, you are well aware that this comment antagonises critics… placing less importance on an interior or a design object than on a work of architecture could be misunderstood. Obviously it implies less responsibility, a lesser impact, yet from the point of view of the cultural process of a project perhaps the approach should always be identical…

The approach is always identical. I am referring to the impact. Getting an architectural project wrong means contributing to the devastation of a territory which anyway up to forty years ago was the most important in the world in terms of its history, tradition and culture. If you get an interior wrong it remains something private let's say.

What are your criteria for judging when a project is wrong? What is your yardstick? You mentioned it being devastating, impacting heavily. But if you had to dictate the rules for getting a work of architecture wrong what would they be?

In architecture there is an axiom used in formulating a project. It is the so-called "genius loci". Today this has been completely lost. Currently we are seeing things which are very beautiful but which I would define more as sculpture than architecture. I, who call myself an architect-art designer who is very connected to the world of contemporary art, am very strict when I design a work of architecture. I do not produce sculptures but things that fit into that place or landscape in terms of the typology, materials used, impact with the context I work in.

Your stance regarding architecture is clear. What do you mean by "art designer"?

My works are one-offs. I do not think of them in terms of industrial production. As soon as a work is a one-off it lies within the boundaries of that "borderline" genre which is art design.

I know you mainly as a creator of projects. You have said that here in Turin there is no investment: "I'm leaving for Milan," you say, but then you go to Berlin, to Copenhagen, to Amsterdam, so you are very Central European too. It is no coincidence you mentioned Vienna. This idea of creating projects and taking them from Italy abroad seems typical of you.

As an Italian who works in art and architecture I can guarantee that as heirs to the world's greatest cultural heritage we still enjoy a great deal of credibility and attention abroad. It is much easier to propose a cultural product outside Italy. There is more interest and it is easier to find the resources to put it into practice. One of the most successful events I designed was "Italian interiors", a show that promoted Italian art design and object art in the world and toured Europe with exhibitions in Prague, Lisbon, Berlin and Copenhagen. It was made possible thanks to the interest that the European and international public has in Italian art products.

Returning to your way of working, the art designer's one-off. You are devising projects and promoting young designers with trade fairs and international concepts. If a company were to come along and say to you "I want you to be my art director", a company that makes products industrially, how would you feel? What would you think?

I have an architect's training, so this kind of offer is one of those work opportunities that can crop up from time to time. I have some experience with art direction in small companies. I worked for Cristal Box, a small company based in Piedmont, in the bathroom sector. For the last Fuorisalone in Milan I designed a collection of lamps called Baby Doll for Fibretec, a company based in Alto Adige.

So you like teamwork. Would you then be willing to coordinate the work of other artists and designers in such a case?

I am interested in the synergy that is created between people working in different creative habitats. There should be more interaction between the world of contemporary art and the world of design and architecture as we saw in the past, such as Ponti with Fornasetti and other important artists of his age. Today these are two separate worlds, the result of that division into sectors which is typical of the contemporary world. I am always surprised when I meet architects who know nothing of contemporary art and vice versa.

Architects and designers who often know nothing of contemporary art. In your opinion why does this happen? Is it not art that isolates itself from a certain field of knowledge?

Contemporary art certainly isolates itself from adjacent habitats and shows no interest in approaching the general public, since the lobbies that control it find this works in their favour. This is evident above all in Italy. However, beyond these motivations it is a question of a lack of cultural bases since contemporary art is missing from school syllabuses where it is needed. It is, above all, missing from university faculties such as architecture where it should be a core subject. Because, anyhow, I consider contemporary art to be a little like Formula 1 compared to mass production, do you understand? It has to be approached with a measure of humility, of modesty. This is why I call myself an "art designer", because doing art is something extremely complex ...

But as an artist you produce one-offs... like the television I see in this room. I am interested in understanding the dynamics that lead you to reinvent a typology, like the great design gurus or architects of the past. What underlies this? Is it divine artistic inspiration or the need to get away from standardisation?

I am the type of person who does not often manage to repeat things. Even when I cook I cannot follow a recipe so I never make the same dish twice... I am unable to replicate anything I do or make... all of this shapes the way I live. I could not bear to have a studio in a fixed place with set working hours. It would make me anxious. My assistants work at home and I am more than happy to hold meetings in the bar. The bar is one of the most creative environments there is in my opinion.

Can I quote a line? You cannot "do" art; you have to "be" an artist.

Perfect. It is an existential dimension. I agree. I have nothing to add to that.

So let's go into detail: not your curriculum though…If you had to describe your work in ten points, from the first thing you did all the way up to the present, be they projects, design objects, architectures or media or outfitting projects, anything.. what would they be?

I would divide my work into different periods. First and foremost, there was the period in Florence where I trained with Professor Gioli and the architectural competitions. Gioli did not force his theories on you but gave you the chance to express yourself albeit within the boundaries of a system of rules. The most significant project dating from this period was the "Ideas Competition" for Jesi Cemetery.

A teacher of critical awareness.

Yes, critical awareness since the architectonic project is based on precise linguistic rules.
This period played a crucial part in my formation due to the powerful design dialectic that developed between the professor and myself.
The second period was the one, once I had disengaged from my teacher, in which I produced my first works of architecture, marked by my winning the IDIA Award, an annual British prize for architecture. I came first in the "Interiors" section with Caravan, a men's clothing store in Alba, a minimal project in which the major protagonist was the space. Indeed, the jury decided to give me the prize for succeeding in producing extremely interesting and efficient forms of space in a very small environment. In fact, my work is realizing spaces. Architecture is space, therefore an interior is space and not decoration. However, the second prize went to Norman Foster... This was important for two reasons: it made me understand that while something of this nature would have been impossible in Italy there was a whole world out there where such a thing was possible, which is very positive and encouraging... and it made me aware of and confident about my way of designing. Finally, there was the period in Turin where I fell under the influences of the great architect Tony Cordero from whom I learned about decoration in terms of manipulating and experimenting with materials as well as involving artists in a project. Cordero invited the gurus of Arte Povera, Merz, Paolini etc. to participate in his works.

Let's move on. You arrive in Turin and begin to work… as an architect? As an art designer? Explain it to me.

Many of my art-design objects are born of my experiences with interiors.

Let's return to here: you are in Turin, art, galleries, work, you haven't told me what percentage of your work is dedicated to making money, not because I want to know how much money you make but how much of your day and your work is dedicated to projects.

I am lucky in the sense that for me work has always been, above all, fun! I have never begun a working relationship where my first thought has been money and then the job in hand. But I can say that when you like something you will probably do it well and make money eventually, too.

You do it well and you make sure it works, because the idea is important. It is important to carry it through to the end but also to make sure the client or your partner understands that what you are doing (and you are doing it well because you are interested in it) may be profitable too.
Yes. However, there has to be a shared idea of the project. That is the most important thing of all. If these necessary preconditions for myself and for the client are not met then there is no point in establishing a working relationship. It may be unproductive from a financial point of view but starting from this principle in my professional life I have never had any negative consequences.

Ah yes. This is symptomatic. It is called "sole rights". It is happening to me too. In similar circumstances I have received similar offers and I have chosen to turn them down on ethical grounds. In a world like the one we live in today, where communication is everything, a person like you, a person like me, if we identify with one reality we are unable then to move elegantly and superficially to another reality. It is not like endorsing a telephone company and then switching to another one once the contract has expired. Ethics, sole rights and identification. What if you were to explain these concepts with your work?
My projects are made-to-measure. In my interiors and, above all, in my projects for homes I am like a tailor who cuts the cloth to fit his customer. Earlier we spoke about the importance of the "genius loci" in architecture. Well, in an interiors project it is just as important to know the client you are working for. It is the only way to produce designs that make sense for both the architect and the client. As Le Corbusier wrote, you are the project's father but the client is the mother... the project has to be built around the client using your own language. It is not an assembly line, do you see? I do one project a year. I have to step inside it, test it, understand it, construct it...

You are introducing an important concept, which is that of time. The designer and the entrepreneur are the historical binomials of Italian design, yet, abandoning the issues of ethics and belonging, there is another factor to consider: time. It is a variable which, in this case, is dependent on and independent of the project, in the sense that you may work on more than one project simultaneously but you require the right amount of time. Let's explain this concept of time in your work better.

Time for me is a huge problem because I am unable to work with maximum intensity on more than one project at a time. It is probably a limitation of mine. I am unable to multitask. When I work on a project I have to throw myself into it. I am not an architect who "forwards" his designs to someone else. I have to realize my own designs. They are a draft which can be referred to when I am on a building site where I plot them with the workman who will build them. I build a work of architecture with others' hands, which is a very different concept to the contemporary way of doing things in which everything is virtual, everything is done by email, architects as well as companies. When I imagine Carlo Scarpa I see him in that famous photo where he is wearing a lab coat and making something with glass. Instead, nowadays many companies have a Starck project in their catalogue but have probably never seen Starck and have only received his designs by email.

What does it mean to be biased nowadays in the world of design? Or rather, after mentioning and explaining the concepts of ethics, belonging, correctness and existentialism of the individual, what does it mean to be biased politically speaking, not in the sense of right or left, but in terms of the project?

Being biased means belonging culturally to the world of those I consider to be my spiritual fathers: Ponti, Albini, Scarpa, Molino... to that generation of architects and to how they experience the project. Obviously my knowledge of them is mediated by my imagination, never having met them personally but knowing them only through their writings and their projects, or through what has been written about them. I cannot know anything about their humanity or whether they were positive or negative people, but it is clear that the way in which Scarpa approached the profession represents an exceptional model of reference. Nowadays, star architects work all over the world on more than one project at a time but often they never enter into the reality in which they work. I work by concentrating on one project at a time. The things that do not interest me or that I am unable to give my full attention to I leave to my co-workers. This is a life choice that probably does not benefit me either economically or professionally. I am not interested in the dimension of the large studio that works on multiple important projects around the world, with dozens of employees who force you into the role of a businessman. It might be a limitation of mine but this is my existential and professional dimension.

I am also unable to delegate or to work with other people if the roles are not clear-cut. I do this and you do that… a very similar temperament influences your behaviour.

Yes, it is a limitation of ours. There are those who manage to handle large commissions because they are able to delegate and organise dozens of people. I cannot do this. It is different kind of job, which does not interest me. Yet it is clear that at this time in history it is a limitation.

So how do you envisage the shared project, with such separate fields of expertise that each person does their own thing?

The shared project for me is a network of people working together. I define the guidelines of a project and then I appoint people with different areas of expertise to develop the themes that the project is made up of. It is a network, as we do not work in a shared space. After an initial briefing everyone develops their own themes, with their own means and in different places and we compare notes and check up on each other by email.

Let's talk about another project. This series, which begins with this volume. It is a project we conceived of as being characterised by an initial conversation, which allows the figure seen in my TV programmes or on other TV programmes to truly emerge.

The synergy that was created between us in this book was very interesting. I had some initial ideas that I was forced to reverse after we had exchanged opinions and this eventually led to a very interesting, dynamic and up-to-date product compared to the one I had imagined. The idea of the conversation came about in order to shake up the standard layout of the architect's book in which works are introduced in their static perfection. Through this conversation we wanted to introduce the person so that their work could be understood.

The ideal project, the one which is consigned to history… Would you like to create a total work of art, to quote a certain German philosopher, or something which marks the territory? What would you like to do that you haven't already done?

One imagines that the ideal project for an architect is a project which marks a city… for me the ideal project might be a small work. A work of architecture may lie within a range that begins with a spoon and ends with a city. The perfect project is not linked to size… it is the "perfect project". It is a question of quality not quantity.

Stand at the sidelines and tell us about some perfect project. Not just one of your own, you may mention other people's projects.

One perfect project is Aldo Rossi's Shutzen-strasse project in Berlin. Indeed, it only makes sense for that building to exist in that context and it can only have been designed by Aldo Rossi.

It is a building that integrates perfectly within the context and is simultaneously recognisable as a unique work created by an extraordinary architect. I think my own perfect projects are Caravan, which we have already mentioned, and a series of works I did in Turin in the early part of the new millennium. These works are a consummate expression of my design poetics, which are the result of my cultural background. The neo-functional starkness of the early works is softened by research into the use and manipulation of materials. Decoration contaminates that spatial starkness which is the result of a functional philosophy.

Let's talk about the clients and the end user, who in theory buys one of your objects, even though we have understood that you do not produce many. How does the client come into this ethical discourse of the project?

The only way is for the client to take part in the realization of the project by becoming an active part of its dialectics. The project should not be an aesthetic model imposed by the architect but a dynamic process that is born of and develops from the interaction between architect and client. The architect interprets and gives a coherent shape to a client's needs, memories and dreams according to his own style-language.

I am writing a book about sustainability in architecture and this is the reason why I have interviewed many luminaries in the field of economics. It seems that, unfortunately, today even Corriere della Sera reiterates the same theory: ethical managers are less in demand than aggressive managers. Is it still the case today that money dictates the rules of a project raising the stakes as it does in the history of art, for obvious reasons and in terms of repositioning?

I think my most interesting projects are those in which I have had access to less funding. The budget can condition you and push you towards an over-decorative representation pandering in some sense to the self-indulgent requests of the client.

Where do you see yourself in twenty years' time?

I try not to see myself in twenty years' time... I see myself in the world. I live in more than one place: Turin where I reside and Tuscany where my roots are. That is what I consider to be my home.

What do you mean by "what I consider to be my home"?

I and my partner Tea, who is an ophthalmologist as well as an artist, buy houses in a bad state of repair and redo them. They are unique pieces, houses I work on patiently and with the attention of a craftsman and where I practically build with my own hands and experiment with materials and ideas. We live in these houses for a time and then we sell them. They are not homes but temporary spaces.

But you were saying where you see yourself in twenty years' time...

I spend periods in Berlin, a city that fascinates me, and in New York, my great passion. At the moment I have four realities, then I will fall in love with another place and move there. There was a time when I was in love with Marrakech and I was there all the time... my life is falling in love, obsessions, temporary transitions, great passions and fierce hatreds.

You are an artist. I'm not an artist. I'm an architect-art designer, which is different...

Walter Vallini

The great Oscar Niemeyer, with a measure of detachment but with a penetrating and authentic vision, insisted that architecture is not so important after all. It is life that is important. It is people and their actions that make the individual. Life choice and the individual, in its highest form, come before any talent or zeal. Vallini must have been in some way inspired by this adage. In the conversation at the beginning of this book he repeatedly upholds this concept. The concept of the quality of life, of the individual who is the faber and who controls the work, or rather varies the pitch of it, without becoming its slave and without settling for compromises in terms of magnificence and opulence.

It is a way of producing architecture that is descended from craftsmanship, informed by the teachings of great architects but based on the practical know-how of the workshop, which today is none other than the art scene. Art is that miraculous mix of ideas and expertise, imbued with stratifications, cultures, inspirations.

There one might start, if one were to trace a profile of Vallini, with his self assigned title of "art designer" and then fill this profile with his projects, which are never identical but always based on the relationship between individuals: the client and the architect/designer. The house is the home of an individual, conceived and made with another individual, and not merely a container of exercises in design.

Giorgio Tartaro

IDIA 1989
INTERIOR DESIGN INTERNATIONAL AWARDS

works 2000 | 2012

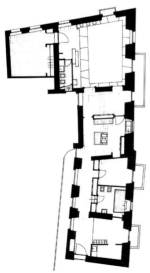

2000

A HOUSE IN TURIN
INTERIOR

2000
FUSION CAFÉ
A LOUNGE BAR IN TURIN
INTERIOR

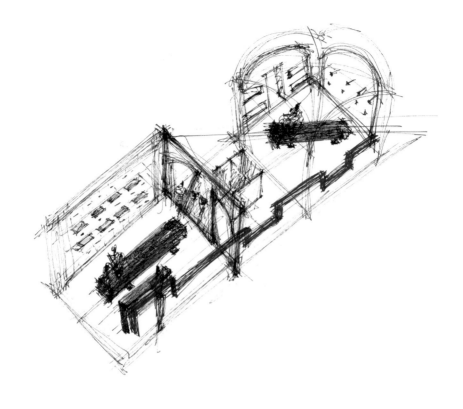

2001

TACCOMANIA
A SHOE STORE IN AOSTA
INTERIOR

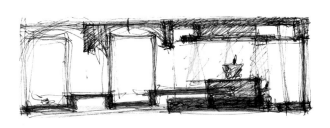

2002

A JEWELRY IN TURIN
INTERIOR

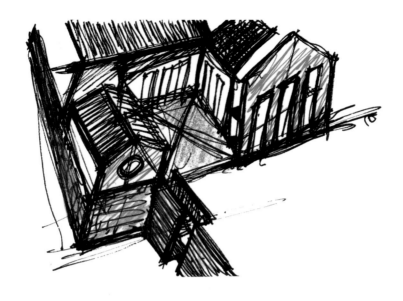

STORAGE WINE CELLAR
+RESTAURANT IN BAROLO
ARCHITECTURE+INTERIOR

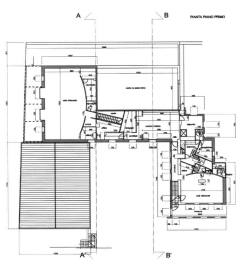

PIANTA PIANO PRIMO

2005
A HOUSE IN TURIN
INTERIOR

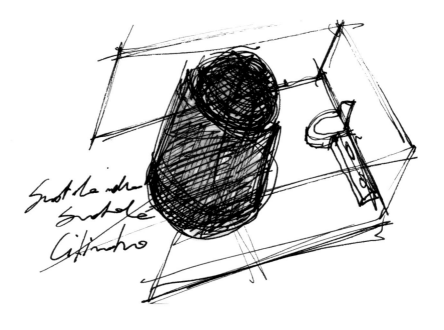

2006

MAISON ARABE
A HAMMAM IN ALBA
INTERIOR

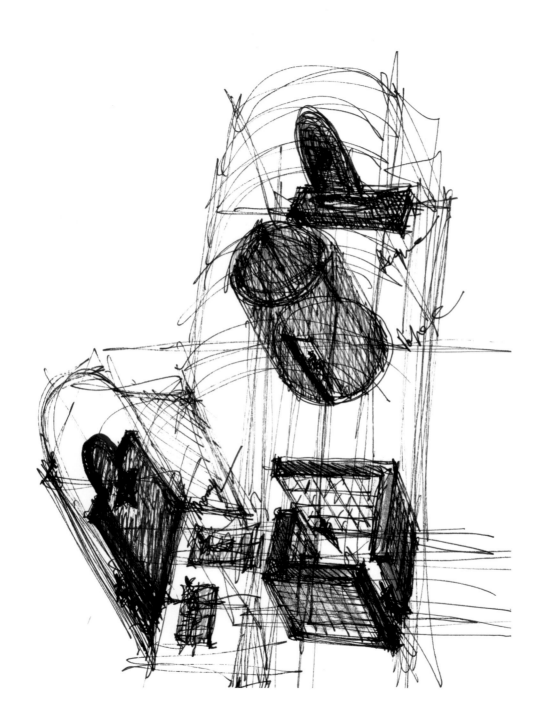

2007
A HOUSE IN TURIN
INTERIOR

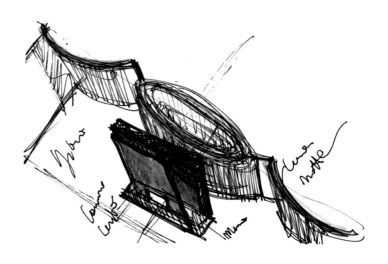

2008

AN APARTMENT IN ST. MORITZ
INTERIOR

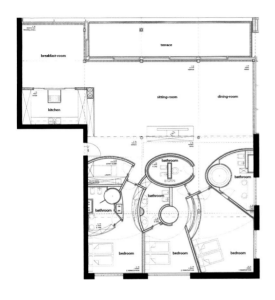

2009
CAFFÉ UMBERTO
WINE BAR IN ALBA
INTERIOR

Assistant Designer
STEFANO VALLINI

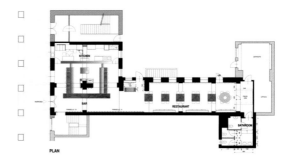

PLAN

2010
A VILLA IN ALBA
ARCHITECTURE+INTERIOR

Assistant Designer
STEFANO VALLINI

A COUNTRY HOUSE IN TUSCANY
INTERIOR

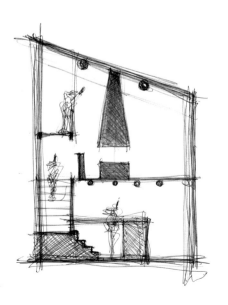

2012

DRIESENERSTRASSE
A STUDIO IN BERLIN
INTERIOR

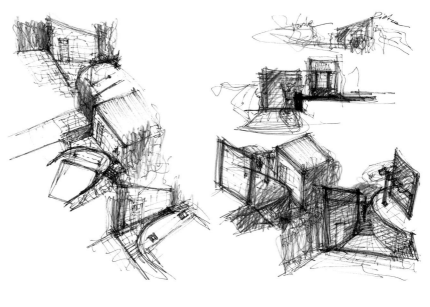

2012

A HOLIDAY HOUSE IN CAVALLO
ARCHITECTURE

Assistant Designer
GIULIA GIROTTO

2002

INTERNI ITALIANI 1 LISBON
EVENTS

BEVISIBLE WITH INVISIBLE
EVENTS

with NELLO TEODORI

1999

L'OGGETTO INUTILE
EVENTS

with GABRIELE SOLUSTRI

Assistant Designer
GIULIA GIROTTO

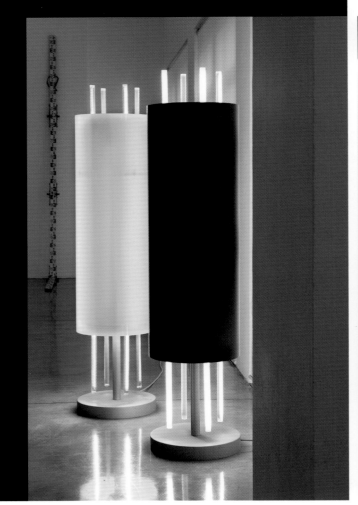

2012

BABYDOLL LAMPS
DESIGN

Assistant Designer
Giulia Girotto

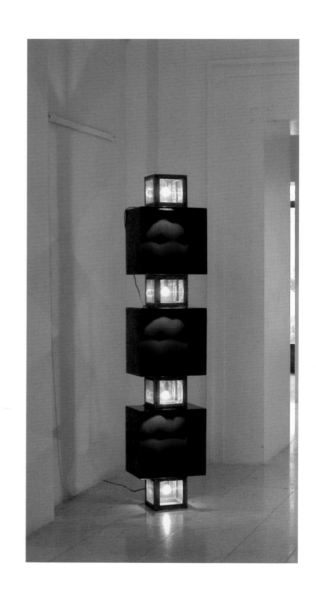

1996

LUMINESCENT BOXES
ART DESIGN

with Michela Formia

2008

BLUE
LUMINESCENT
BOOKSHELVES
ART DESIGN

2012

REDS OF THE MIND
NEW YORK
INSTALLATION

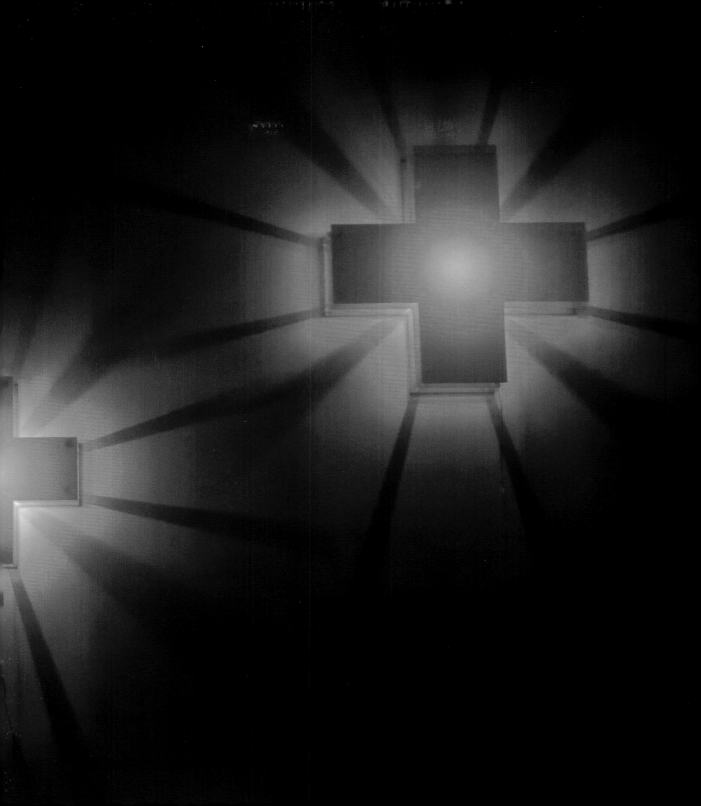

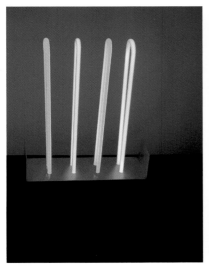

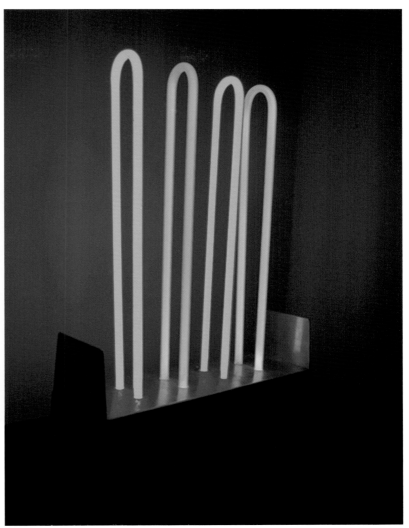

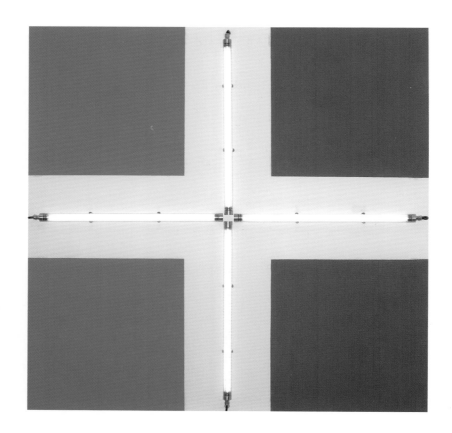

2012

VIVA L'ITALIA
ART DESIGN

2012

THE REALM OF LIGHT
STUDIO 303 NY

EXHIBITION

96 | **97**

2008

EXIT
LAMP
ART DESIGN

2006

NO CITY LIMIT
LUMINESCENT TABLE
ART DESIGN

with SILVANO COSTANZO

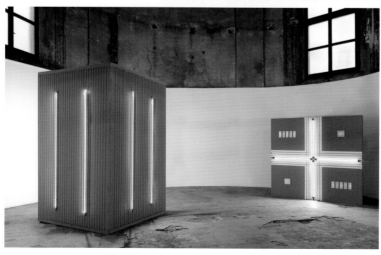

2011
**W L'ITALIA
MILANO**
INSTALLATION

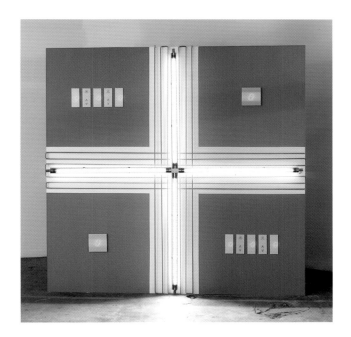

2011
SIAMO SVIZZERI PAISÀ
MILANO
INSTALLATION

AWARDS

1993

2°Award Absolute
by Ideal Standard - Milan

1989

IDIA Awards - London

MAIN PUBLICATIONS

2012

Living in Lift exhibition catalogue:
"Living in Lift Atto terzo" pp. 10-11
"Walter Vallini" pp. 69-70

Territorio Uomo Territorio
exhibition catalogue

The Realm of Light
exhibition catalogue

CASE & STILI - September 2012:
"I Protagonisti - Walter Vallini"

*Padiglione Italia at the 54t*ʰ *Venice
Art Biennale* exhibition catalogue:
"Walter Vallini"

2011

*Un'altra storia. Arte Italiana dagli
anni Ottanta agli anni Zero* exhibition catalogue:
"Walter Vallini" pp.188-189

Living in Lift exhibition catalogue:
"Living in Lift o le visioni di un archi-
tetto" pp.12-14
"Walter Vallini opere" pp. 61-65

2010

BRAVA CASA - December 2010:
"Giochi d'equilibrio" pp. 108-117

IQD INSIDE QUALITY DESIGN July/
September 2010:
"L'equilibrio di contrapposizioni
dialettiche" pp. 124-127

BAGNO ACCESSORI - August/
September 2010:

"Raffinato ed insolito contrasto di
colori" pp. 72-77

A-Z 2 ARCHITECTURE ZONE 2 -
RIHAN.cc:
"Lo Zoccolaio" pp. 310-312

DDB 52:
"Contrasti geometrici nella linearita'
dello spazio" pp. 90-98

*Anni Zero - Arte Italiana del nuovo
decennio* exhibition catalogue:
" Walter Vallini Red and Blue"

MAXIMA INTERIORES n°107 -
February 2010:
"Italiano para principiantes"
pp. 82-90

FASHIONTREND-MAGAZINE -
June 2010:
"Milano design week 2010
bevisible+atnhowhotel"

2009

IDEAT n°69:
"A turin Revolution de palace"
pp. 174-181

MARIE CLAIRE MAISON - October
2009:
"Armonia dei Contrasti"
pp. 102-112

TITOLO n°60 - Autumn 2009:
"Gianni Asdrubali, Tea Giobbio,
Walter Vallini - Trittongo" p. 52

SPACE x FILE commercial space vol.
02 - RIHAN.cc:

"Maison Arabe" pp. 20-21

*Triennale della Ceramica d'Arte
Contemporanea di Gualdo Tadino*
exhibition catalogue:
"Walter Vallini" pp. 68-69

TO.7 LA STAMPA ARTE -
16th January 2009:
"Da Fusion Arts le creazioni di
Fukushi, Guzzetti, Micheli, Sottsass,
Deodori, Vallini. Lavori d'arte e
oggetti di design per il piacere
d'abitare nelle case" p. 13

2008

TORINO TOUR *la guida definitiva
visual design per una città invisibile:*
"11 CRIBI'"

*1° Biennale Internazionale d'Arte
Contemporanea- Sabbioneta 2008*
exhibition catalogue:
"Walter Vallini" pp. 130-131

ELLE DECORATION 6 -
Oct/Nov 2008:
"Tiefe Tone" pp. 156-165

IL GIORNALE DELL'ARCHITETTURA
June 2008:
"Monografia Abitare il Tempo"

5+5 exhibition catalogue, Alinea,
Florence 2008:
"Cascina lo Zoccolaio" F. Arese
Visconti pp. 14-17
"Maison Arabe" M. Bignamini
pp. 18-21
"Cascina lo Zoccolaio" M. Franci
pp. 22-26

ARTE Mondadori - September 2008:
"A Sabbioneta le formule di 32
artisti" pp.192-193

2007

IL BAGNO OGGI E DOMANI n°235
October 2007:
"Il colore viola" pp. 128-133

RIABITA n°5 - May 2007:
"La ristrutturazione di un appartamento a Torino" pp. 9-15

DDN MAGAZINE n°138:
"Oggetti Luminosi & Dialoghi
Incrociati"

2006

New Restaurants 2, L'Archivolto,
Milan 2006:
"Locanda nel borgo antico"
pp. 86-91

*BAM Free Zone
Biennale d'arte moderna e contemporanea del Piemonte 2006*
exhibition catalogue:
"Walter Vallini & Vittorio Valente"
p. 109

Stairs-Scale 2, L'Archivolto, Milan
2006:
"Walter Vallini" p. 114

2005

Fireplaces-Camini, L'Archivolto,
Milan 2005:
"W.Vallini" pp. 124-125

2004

LA STAMPA 28/3/2004:
Giorno e Notte "Dal Quadrilatero a
Copenaghen" p. 51

JP KOBENHAVN 31/12/2004:
Kultur Weekend "Italierwe taender
lyset" p. 13

2003

OFX n°70 - February 2003:
"Fusion Cafe' Galleria d'arte e architettura - gallery of art and architecture" pp. 158-161

DDB5:
"Bagno viola" pp. 82-87

Berlin 2003 - Interni Italiani 3
exhibition catalogue

2002

MID EDICOES DIMENSAO -
3rd quarter 2002:
"Exposicao Interni Italiani" noticia
events noticias

Bathrooms-Bagni, L'Archivolto,
Milan 2002:
"28 Walter Vallini" pp. 72-74
"21 Michela Formia - Walter Vallini"
pp. 56-57

New Shops 7, L'Archivolto, Milan
2002:
"Taccomania" pp. 12-17
"Giobbio Gioielli" pp. 208-213

MODO n° 223 - Oct/Nov 2002:
Proscenio "Interni Italiani" p.18

IL BAGNO OGGI E DOMANI
March 2002:
"Elogio della diagonale" pp. 76-79

ARTE Mondadori n° 349
September 2002:
"Interni Italiani otto autori tra arte e
design" p. 122

Una Babele Postmoderna
exhibition catalogue, Mazzotta,
Milan 2002:
"Progetto di Allestimento" p. 31

DDB1 DESIGN DIFFUSION
BATHROOM:
"Blu intenso, minimale ed esotico"
pp. 116-119

DDB3 DESIGN DIFFUSION
BATHROOM:
"Elogio della diagonale due bagni a
Torino" pp. 96-99

Praga 2002 - interni italiani italske'interie'ry exhibition catalogue:
"Interni Italiani 2 - Oltre Milano,
design ed altro"
"Walter Vallini"

2000

Urban Interiors 3, L'Archivolto,
Milan 2000:
"Colore Emozionale-Touching Color"
pp. 204-209

IL BAGNO OGGI E DOMANI n°182
March 2000:
"Etnico Metropolitano" pp. 78-81

1997

CASA & GIARDINO
Dec. 1997/Jan.1998:
"in un appartamento ad Alba elementi disegnati e calde tonalità del
legno" pp. 38-44

INTERNI - September 1997:
"Abitare il Tempo" p. 88

Nuovo Allestimento Italiano, Lybra,
Milan 1997:
"Allestire negozi" pp. 38-43

Nuovi Negozi in Italia 4, L'Archivolto,
Milan 1997:
" Cribi" pp. 26-29
" Sussurri e grida" p. 1

1995

Nuove Abitazioni in Italia 2, L'Archivolto, Milan 1995:
"Successioni Domestiche-Domestic
Succession" pp. 58-65

Nuovi Negozi in Italia 3, L'Archivolto,
Milan 1995:
"Vassallo Gioielli" pp. 12-15

1994

Nuovi Negozi in Italia 2, L'Archivolto,
Milan 1994:
"Maria Gallo" pp. 202-205

1993

*Nuove Abitazioni in Italia: Nuovi
Ambienti Italiani*, L'Archivolto, Milan
1993:
"Walter Vallini"

1992

SHOP DESIGN EUROPEAN MASTERS:
"Caravan" pp. 94-101
"M. Gallo" pp. 102-109

1991

MD n°4 - April 1991:
"Boutique in Alba" pp. 78-79

1990

DOMUS 7 15th April 1990:
"Negozio caravan ad Alba" pp. 1-3

World Space Design 02, edited by
the Moriyama Editors Studio:
"Caravan" pp.12-15

Nuovi Negozi in Italia, L'Archivolto,
Milan 1990:
"Caravan" pp. 14-15
"Donne Vincenti" pp. 16-17

1989

Interior Design - June 1989:
IDIA 1989 "Putting the Caravan
First" p. 59

MAIN EXHIBITIONS

2013

Living in Lift
15th March CAMeC Centro Arte
Moderna e Contemporanea,
La Spezia

2012

*The realm of light. Tea Giobbio and
Walter Vallini*
20th September - Studio 303,
New York

2011

*"Un'Altra Storia. Arte Italiana dagli
anni Ottanta agli anni Zero"*
16th September - CRAB Centro
Ricerca Accademia di Brera - Ex
Chiesa di S. Carpoforo, Milan

"Living in Lift"
15th December - CRAB Centro
Ricerca Accademia di Brera - Ex
Chiesa di S. Carpoforo, Milan

*"Padiglione Italia alla 54° Esposi-
zione Internazionale d'Arte della
Biennale di Venezia"*
17th December - Palazzo delle
Esposizioni Sala Nervi, Turin

2009

*"Triennale della Ceramica d'Arte
Contemporanea di Gualdo Tadino"*
30th May - Chiesa di S. Francesco,
Gualdo Tadino (Pg)

"Trittongo"
3rd October - Wunderkammern,
Rome

2008

"5+5 artisti+architetti"
16th April - Museu da Agua, Lisbon

"5+5 artisti+architetti"
24th May - Galeria do Palacio Biblio-
teca Almeida, Garrett Port

*"1°Biennale Internazionale d'Arte
Contemporanea"*
31st August - Palazzo Ducale Sabbioneta (Pr)

2007

*"Fatto ad Arte-Territori di Ceramica
Italiana Contemporanea-Ceramica
Umbra"*
25th June - Musei di S. Salvatore in
Lauro, Rome

2006

"Breakfast Design"
18th March - Gewerbe Museum,
Winterthur

*"Oggetti Luminosi & Dialoghi
Incrociati"*
19th October - Galeria de Exposico-
es do ISCTE, Lisbon

"Intersezioni 6+6"
17th November - G Space, Venice

2005

"Furniture of Mind"
8th February - Boutique Borsalin,
Paris

2004

*"Oggetti Luminosi & Dialoghi
Incrociati"*
3rd December - Istituto Italiano di
Cultura, Copenhagen

2003

"Interni Italiani 3"
24th June - Tacheles Kunsthaus,
Berlin

2002

"Interni Italiani 1"
9th April - Sociedade Nacional de
Belas Artes, Lisbon

"Interni Italiani 2"
10th October - St. Borromeo Cha-
pel, Prague

ACKNOWLEDGEMENTS

I would like to thank Tea Giobbio, Davide Lovati and Adriana Toti for their support.

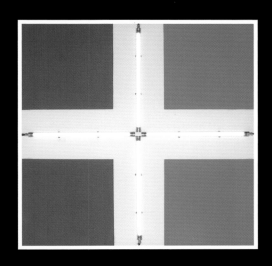